Elijah Power

Rev Steve Gaskins

ISBN: 978-1-67811-373-5

Eric & Joanie

May God bless you all
the days of your life

Steve Gaskins

Elijah Power

Rev Steve Gaskins

Other Titles by Steve Gaskins:

This is my first book, but I have 3 books I'm working on;

Genesis Series Book 1: Beginnings
From pre-creation through the great flood to Abram. Includes Lucifer's rebellion, creation, Garden of Eden, Fall of Man, Cain and Able, Noah, and the tower of Babble.

Luke Series Book 1: Birth
God's choice of Mary and Joseph, Birth of John the Baptist, and Birth and youth of Jesus

12 Tribes
Twelve brothers make 13 tribes (Joseph is divided between his two sons) and they are referred to at different times in the bible in different orders announcing the situation they are in.

Steve Gaskins

ISBN: 978-1-67811-373-5

First Printing edition 2020

Walking with Jesus Ministry

PO Box 131

Oologah OK 74053

WalkingWithJesus@GMX.com

WWW.Walking-With-Jesus.com

Dedicated

To my sons Allen, Steven, Thomas, and David
To my daughters Belinda and Allyanna

These are the six best reason I have for doing
anything,
I pray for them and the world they will encounter.

Table of Contents

BONUS

Elijah Power

Steve Gaskins

CHAPTER ONE
WHEN GOD IS SILENT

So then faith cometh by hearing,
and hearing by the word of God.
Romans 10:17

IT IS THE mid-1990s and I am sitting in a small church in Owasso Oklahoma across the street from where my soon-to-be wife grew up. I am in my early 30s and have just recently returned to the church. I grew up in the church with my mom playing piano and dad trying to keep me from wiggling out of my chair; Vacation Bible School (VBS) with friends, church camps, getting baptized with water at 12 and baptized with the Holy Spirit at 17. At 20 I joined the US Air Force as a chapel manager where I became active with teens and got my first real taste of church politics. Here I am trying to listen to a preacher who exudes love for the 20-or-so members of this church. When he has us bow our heads to pray, I take the usual position which I have known all my life … head down, eyes closed, feel the presence of God with me as I do some lame prayer … this time there's a problem. As I began to pray, I suddenly felt very alone, there was no comforting presence of God which I have taken for granted all these years. I have known about my having a calling on my life, but I felt there was no reason to rush toward my calling because God will always patiently wait … not this morning … GOD IS NOT HERE! We say amen and I get up and start walking toward the door; I shake the preacher's hand and walk straight to the car. I AM SCARED! Has God given up on me? Have I pressed my luck for too long and He has finally found someone more willing to serve? Yeah, yeah, I know I'm going to Heaven but what about my calling … did I blow it? I went home and got very serious about my attitude and God. I began praying earnestly and guess who showed up … God was there, and He has always been there except one small time when He withheld his presence and got my attention.

One prayer of one young man, imagine a people who have not heard an answer from God for generations. Enters Moses after 400 years of nothing and a multitude of prayers lifted up from slaves. This is the same God who had been so close to the founder Abraham, had saved Isaac, and had shown Jacob the ladder to Heaven. God has been quietly sitting on the throne while the people became complacent and then apathetic. They prayed out of habit with no belief in their prayers being heard. Here comes the murderous prince out of exile who after several decades in the desert decides he's a messenger for the God who has been silent for over 4 centuries. Like many in desperate times there are those who rush to him with his story of help but there are others who are less trusting. His first great act is to make the masters mad at the Jewish people and cause them to no longer get their straw to make bricks … thanks a lot Moses. The number of followers has now dwindled to a remnant who has been praying to a God who refused to reply. One miracle after another happens, and each time the true believers rejoice, the apathetic scoff, and the

middle watch and wait. Finally, God has Pharaoh release them just so Pharaoh can try to kill them in the desert. Pharaoh's army pushes them against the Red Sea, but a pillar of smoke or fire holds them back from their task. Finally, God releases Pharaoh and his army in a blind rage to follow a people across a dry seabed with water held back on both sides. Then God shows his greatness by destroying the greatest army on earth and its leader, Pharaoh. After seeing 10 plagues effect Egypt but not Goshen, after walking across a dry sea bed and watching God hold back the armies until everyone is safe then closing the sea on the army, you'd think the people would be earnestly God's people … but no. Moses goes up the mountain for 30 days and they decide that God is not real and Moses is dead … we need a golden calf. God opens up the earth and swallows the unbelievers and begins feeding the faithful some manna from Heaven. Since the true apathetic people are gone and miracles actually happen on a daily basis except on Friday when a special miracle happens; the food is good for 2 days (Friday and Shabbat) instead of 1 … this

crew is ready to follow God to the ends of the earth … but no. They get to the promise land and it's not handed to them on a silver platter, there is food and water just waiting for them to come get it but there are also giants. These giants weren't able to defeat Pharaoh's army which perished in the sea by God's hand, but the children of Abraham can't trust God to get rid of the giants. The complaint was God had been silent and now God has been anything but silent and yet many believe Moses is just a charismatic ex-royal who is hearing voices. It took 40 years in the desert and a generation who had known nothing but hardship to get the people ready for God's blessing.

Jump forward 1,100 years and David was a great king who spoke with God through prophets and his son Solomon did as well in the beginning but they're both dead and have been for about 100 years. Israel has been split into two kingdoms and this one has an evil king and a wicked queen who established her gods, Baal and Asherah, in the capital and made 850 priests while killing or sending into hiding all the priest of God. The people are happy bowing to the royals and their gods, keeping up appearances. They would say things like Jehovah was my grandparent's god, I have the new and hip Baal to worship because I'm modern. Along comes Elijah who begins irritating the royal couple. To start with Elijah locks up the water to the country for 3 ½ years and then takes a cloud the size of a man's hand and makes a downpour. During the drought he takes off and lives with a widow woman where he makes her a cruse of unending oil to go with her barrel of unending meal for so long as the drought lasts. He raised the widow's son from the dead and he was fed by ravens and by an angel; yet the people were more concerned with following trends than following God. It was when God lit a fire and Elijah killed the priests of the false gods that the people began getting serious about following God.

Jump another 900 years and we have a people who have not heard from God in almost 500 of those years. The people have become a conquered people again. The halls of the synagogue are filled with corrupt priests and the yards are filled with apathy.

Thieves rule the temple while boasting how they are so very religious, but in fact they have spliced God's word so finely it allowed them to legally steal. The people of God go to the holy city and have to buy from merchants, who price goods extremely high because there is no choice but to purchase from them (if you chose to bring your own offering the priest would say it is unacceptable to God). The people are under oppression from Rome but again they have not heard from God. There is a remnant of faithful followers, but they are greatly outnumbered by the others. They try to give God's word but are scorned by the wicked and disbelieved by the people: if they don't go into hiding, they are often killed or relegated to some small town in the middle of nowhere. John comes along with a couple of miracles in his birth to be scorned and sent out away from the main men. He has a small following willing to endure a great deal of hardship to reach him, but to those who come, there is a blessing. He does not part the sea nor raise the dead; he declares the true word of God. He will lead them to Jesus, who will lead them to God the father and His righteousness.

CHAPTER TWO
THE POWER OF THREE

Him God raised up the third day, and shewed him openly;

Acts 10:40

GOD LOVES THE NUMBER THREE. He has given much power to three and we who are in His image have followed suit by giving a lot of things three parts. There are three in the trinity of God (Father, Son, Holy Spirit), the Ark of the Covenant has 3 items in it (a gold jar of manna, Aaron's staff which had budded, and the stone tablets of the covenant) and there are three holy feasts (Unleavened Bread, Weeks, and Tabernacles). In America we have three branches of government and three parties (Republican, Democrat, Independent). There are three churches (Catholic, Protestant, Eastern Orthodox), We understand that each of the three has many parts but we like having our clusters in threes. Israel had the same in the synagogue

(Sadducees, Pharisees, and Independents) but we refer to the people of Israel as one people just like we call the three parties of Americans as one people and the three churches as the church.

There is one other three I want to share before I go deep into this part. The three distinct groups within the church. They break down through which of the Trinity they pursue the most and as such their worship differs. Those who pursue God the Father primarily are rich in tradition and often more ceremony than spontaneity. You will recognize them quickly because they have the sacraments in the middle of the stage area and the preacher/priest is usually off to one side and often there will be another lectern on the other side for the scripture reading by a laity. The second group pursues God the Son, our Lord Jesus the Christ primarily and are set with hymns and sermons from the gospels; they center around the life and ministry of Jesus. The pulpit is in the center of the stage because the Word is the primary focus of the church. The final group pursues God the Holy Spirit primarily and they enjoy the spontaneity of a service. You will often hear their pastor say how God changed his sermon and the pulpit may be to the side with the piano in the center of the stage. As with any set we will find one group that has tendencies of another just like we will find conservative Democrats and protestants who believe in confessing to the pastor. This also does not include sects. With that being said; let us continue with our discussion.

We will be addressing four groups of threes; there are three types of people we will talk about throughout this booklet. There are three groupings that we will address concerning three aspects of the Spirit of Elijah which will culminate into the three Powers of Elijah. The three types of people are: 1. Lovers of God 2. Lovers of sin and 3. Those who try to ride the fence. The three groupings of people are: 1. The church as a whole 2. Leadership within the local church (pastors, deacons, evangelist, and others) and 3. The individual Christian. Some comments may hit home and some may seem strange because they do not reflect your situation ... remember church politics are often played out behind closed doors and many in the congregation have no idea what trouble is brewing in the pastor's office. The three aspects of the spirit of Elijah are: 1. Uncompromising truth 2. A disturbing healing of the soul and 3. Creating a path for one who is greater. These three spirits will create the three powers of Elijah: 1. Turning the hearts of fathers to their children 2. Turning the hearts of children to their fathers and 3. Turning the hearts of the people to God through repentance.

The three types of people often break into three groups 1. Those who are forthwith about who they are 2. Those who are cleverly disguised and 3. Those who are borderline or simply misguided.

Lovers of God: The forthwith ones are fantastic and often rejoiced by those whom they know or are known, Mother Theresa and Billy Graham are great examples. There are others who are less known but to those who are close to them they are superstars. I have known some missionaries who risk great things to serve God, there are pastors and deacons in constant prayer seeking a way to

Steve Gaskins

present God to the people. They are often involved in charities or working with homeless, unwed mothers, AIDS victims, abused people, and many others. There are some great teachers whom God has granted insight and musicians who touch the soul for God. These lovers of God have a glorious place in God's kingdom. What about the lovers of God who are disguised? 1 Kings 18: 3&4 "And Ahab called Obadiah, which was the governor of his house. (Now Obadiah feared the Lord greatly: For it was so, when Jezebel cut off the prophets of the Lord, that Obadiah took a hundred prophets, and hid them in fifty in a cave, and fed them with bread and water)." So there are those who are in a place of evil who serve the Lord while obeying the evil commands. We in America are hard pressed because we can just quit when we want to leave a situation but there are many in the world who cannot leave so they become disguised. I remember meeting some Bible runners back in the early 2000s who disguised themselves to bring God's word to the communist nations. Finally, we have those who are borderline, they love God more than mammon, but

21

they can't seem to get it right. I told my friend Archiel Spencer Jr. about academic Christians. They were raised in a church of morals, went to a Bible college of morals, and love to quote scripture but their faith is no better than their memorization of math formulas. God will bless them for their desire to love Him but they can't seem to bridge the gap between studied information and a relationship with a person. It's like a piano player who can hit every note perfectly but has no emotion in their playing.

Lovers of sin: The forthwith ones are often in prison because their actions are so contrary to common care, society has decided they cannot walk among us. There are those who are cruel and cause others to commit sins like pimps and drugs dealers who get women addicted to the drugs and then they turn them into prostitutes: rapist who breaks into a home to terrorize the family, murderers and pedophiles. This is not a confused view of the world but a hatred of innocence, joy, and peace. The disguised ones are often in the church or civic organizations. The racist judge or cop, the doctor who admitted to giving Jews the wrong medicine hoping to kill them or at least making them miserable, the doctor who always suggests abortion or assisted suicide to those hurting. The pastor who says I believe in God but not the Bible. There is a man who has pastored several churches in the Collinsville Oklahoma area who has split every church he has pastored. There are men who tickle the ears of the deacons with promises of forthcoming wealth but needs a different preacher or tickles the ear of the preacher but will not bring it where certain people attend. I call it the spirit of Absalom, for he sat at the gate saying "if I was king" turning people away from David hoping to create enough discord where he could become king. The misguided are plentiful ... they are pursuing the three tools the devil loves: power, wealth and fame. You can find them roaming the halls of congress (both in office and trying to influence those in office), on and off Broadway or in Manhattan high rises in New York, Hollywood, San Francisco, TV shows and news, slum lords, mayors, councilmen, con men, thieves, strippers, prostitutes, and some are in the church.

Fence sitters: Some are often near or beside the misguided lovers of sin. They are in church but they're eyes are still a little glazed from Saturday night's activities. Their struggle with sin is fighting their desire to be a good person. I have a friend who had a horrible roller coaster fight with drugs; he would be good for a while and be in church with his wife and children then he would disappear for a few months while his habit killed his job and robbed him of his relationship with God. It's the drug dealer who thinks tithing makes the rest of the money good. The deceptive ones are aggressive and well spoken, they teach Sunday school or even stand in the pulpit. I love that a couple of the people in the left behind series are a preacher and a piano player at the church. They can be a bishop or cardinal. Who would have guessed so many of the priests had been pedophiles? The misguided are busy with work, home, kids, and just enjoying their lives, not hurting anyone with their moral lives.

Martin Luther King Jr wrote from the Birmingham jail to the preachers in the town saying he must confess that the white moderate, or what we call the liberal bystander today, is too busy making appeasement arguments to effect change. He believed that the path to equality wasn't blocked by the hate groups like the White Citizens Councillor or the Ku Klux Klan, but it was the wait for change encouraged by the white moderates and their allies amongst the black community that did not want to cause trouble. He said that the white moderate was more concerned with order than justice, that they would prefer negative peace (the absence of tension) to a positive peace (the presence of justice). He accused them of agreeing with his goal but disagreeing with his methods of direct action. He said that they want to set a timetable for another man's freedom by encouraging them to "wait for a better season" It was a shallow understanding from people with good intentions, and it was more frustrating than hateful misunderstanding from people with bad intentions. Jesus said a Lukewarm makes him sick because lukewarm acceptance is much more bewildering than outright rejection.

Notes

CHAPTER THREE
UNCOMPROMISING TRUTH

*So shall my word be that goeth forth out of my mouth: it
shall not return unto me void, but it shall accomplish that
which I please, and it shall prosper in the thing whereto I
sent it.* Isaiah 55:11

THE UNCOMPROMISING TRUTH OF GOD'S WORD has
no room for gray. The people on Mt. Carmel were asked
how long they would continue to halt between two
opinions (1 King 18:21) while Jesus said we cannot serve
two masters (Matt 6:24). There is no gray here, you are all
in or all out. Jesus called those with one foot in and one
foot out something so horrible it makes him spew (vomit)
(Rev 3:16). That is in distinct contrast with the world today
where everything is considered based on a nuance. Is
killing a baby in the womb wrong? What if it is deformed

and will never live unless attached to machines? Is killing wrong? What if it's the state killing a murderer? Is it wrong for powerful men to take advantage of gold diggers and is it any of our business? The world used to be a lot simpler when John Wayne would play a character who gave his word and had no use for nuances. The world was not perfect, but it seemed a lot more cut and dry. The town square could display the manger scene, kids played baseball and if they got into a disagreement there might be a black eye involved. If a black eye happened, we did not call the police and sue for damages. Not everyone was happy but that hasn't changed ... there are just as many unhappy people today as then. Don't get me wrong, I'm glad we have changed some of the bigotry from back then: we allow everyone to sit together and use the same bathrooms. We don't lynch people or block the way into schools. OH YEAH, there was one other big difference back then: The preacher stood in front of the congregation and spoke clearly about things like the sanctity of life and the damnation of those who do not know Jesus. Today the number one discussion from the pulpit is what Jesus has and can do for you and not what your commitment should be to Jesus. Nothing wrong with making Jesus more accessible but we cannot avoid the wrath of God without people thinking its ok if I choose not to follow one path. Hell is still just as real and there are just as many trying to lead people there ... including those in the church who don't think it's a big deal.

There is NO GRAY!!! There is repentance and reconciliation but there is no gray. If God's word says don't be an adulterer and you are dating a married woman ... REPENT. I don't care if her husband is mean, until she is released from her vows and prepared to take new ones ... Leave it alone. I knew a chaplain in the Air Force, if he knew the General was having an affair, not only would he not preach against it, but he would find a way to justify it. THERE IS NO GRAY!!! That is not to say we should have our churches caught up in the weeds of legalism, but rather we should not bow our message to appease this world, the power players in the church, the chief donators, or anyone else ... Preach to God and let the congregation listen in ... if they get upset, let them discuss it with God because he's tired of hearing sermons preached to the congregation and finding out how much sugar water was added to make it where they wouldn't get offended.

There should be uncompromising truth in the church. Here a while back the Baptist convention simply stated they believe Ephesians chapter 5 is what God meant to say and they agree with God. The world went crazy and the news outlets brought forth every preacher they could find to criticize the Baptist … but this wasn't a Baptist principle but the word of God these pastors were criticizing. So how many other things have we as a church decided we're too evolved to follow in God's word: women pastors (1Tim 2:12) or appointing deacons due to the wealth of offering instead of a wealth of Godly knowledge (1Tim 3:6). We do not have a great overseer in the protestant church like the Pope, but we do have the ability as a group to support those who are biblical and to separate ourselves from those who are not biblical. We have had no problem ostracizing the Westboro Baptist Church because their actions are against God's word. Let the denominations and the non-denominational churches set a standard that must be upheld, or face being ostracized as a sect.

Speaking of non-denominational churches, it has been fashionable for a preacher who disagrees with denominational rules to start a non-denominational church. This is not very different from when preachers would go West to plant a church amongst the heathens; whether the heathens were Indians, cattlemen, gold or silver miners, or the wild and wooly townspeople who helped them spend their money. Non-denominational churches differ from denominational churches that dominated the East coast in years gone by and were also dominant in twentieth-century America. My favorite story of a denominational split is the Church of God of Prophesy split from the Assembly of God because they couldn't abide with second marriages (and still can't). There are several variations of Baptist, Methodist, and so forth but generally the denominational name will hold certain characteristics. Whether it's Freewill or Southern Baptist, you probably won't hear speaking in tongues. The non-denominational churches primarily started with a pastor wanting a charismatic church (speaking in tongues, healing through laying on of hands, casting out demons, dancing in the aisles) and could not find a denomination that would accept such activities. The charismatic churches are almost a denomination unto themselves. With that said, the freedom the pastors found has also created some cross-bearing buildings where Christ is not spoken. Some crazy understandings of the Bible include preachers who say God is love and the rest of the Bible is written by men and has no bearing on what is true. This freedom to start a non-denominational church is also missing some of the structure that creates accountability. Deacon boards are often filled with yes men to either the pastor or the head deacon (who is all too often the biggest financial supporter of the church). When the pastor goes off the rails into non-biblical territory, there is no one there with the authority to stop him. So, let's deal with the local churches and pastors who desire to teach Jesus Christ and him crucified (1 Cor 2:2).

There are many great missionaries, evangelist, pastors, deacons, worship leaders, teachers, and prayer warriors within the local church. The reason we still have a Christian foundation to this nation is not because of the megachurch but because of the family church that refuses to compromise. As people have moved into the cities for work and away from the small towns scattered throughout the nation, we are seeing family churches dwindle and die. To offset the loss of family ties to bring in new members, many pastors are softening their message to attract younger members. The music is becoming more upbeat; the sermons are more about the rewards on earth rather than about being a good steward. The shift in population has forced many changes in business practices and it needed to make some shifts in the church. The city may not have three generations of a family in one small area but the old adage, birds of a feather flock together, still applies. People in a certain area of the larger towns and cities have something in common and want a local church serving that commonality. Some areas are blue collar or middle income while other areas are posh high maintenance people. There are four gospels because even the young under-educated disciples understood that different people needed to see a different aspect of the same Christ. The gospels did not tell of a different man, the core always stayed true to the man, but one is about a suffering servant while another was about the fulfillment of prophecy. The two questions for every church are 1. are you serving your community as it is or as you wish it was? And 2. If a person from a different church walked into your church would they recognize the same Jesus? Do they know Jesus as some guy walking through the money changers table with one hand in his coat and mildly turning over tables or do they see a man so enraged by the religious people selling God and cheating His people that he physically made a whip and began driving them out? Is Jesus moved by compassion or following a script when dealing with those lost, hurt, and afraid? The uncompromising truth doesn't always have to be harsh, but it must be complete. Jesus, like most of us, has the hard side a father often presents to make his children obey and gives them comfort because no bully can come into their house when their dad is home, but he also has the soft side that tucks in a sick child and reads him a book or plays catch and wants to be a part of his life. Too many churches today show the soft side without the side that demands obedience and respect.

We do not discipline our children because we hate them … just the opposite, as mature adults we understand; being harsh today will keep our children out of danger tomorrow. The same is true with the Word of God: If we do not teach our congregations about God's wrath, they will feel it in the future. It is far better to hurt feelings today than an eternity in Hell because a pastor didn't want to offend anyone. This is no joking matter, but we have raised a generation who thinks it's funny.

Notes

CHAPTER FOUR

DISTURBING HEALING OF THE SOUL

Whoever loves instruction loves knowledge,
But he who hates correction is stupid. Prov 12:1

OFTEN THE JOB OF A PROPHET is to move people out of their comfort zone so they can be used by God in a new way. "Comfort zone" is a common phrase in America, it's referred to as the box (think outside the box), the rut, the place where we know well and are not afraid. It's the third seat from the end on aisle 4 ... not too close to the pastor and not too far back among the sleepers. It's a $20 or $100, we don't give a tithe we give a denomination of dollars easy to fold. It's the casserole dish of life ... easy to throw together, stick in the oven, and present to our friends with little or no effort: Everyone likes it so why change.

When a man is drowning it is said a calmness falls over him so that he drifts to sleep and dies. When a man is freezing to death, he has the same kind of feeling as his body becomes numb and he just wants to go to sleep until the end. But if he goes to sleep he will perish in his comfort. When a rescuer comes he has to startle the person out of their restful state to save their life. They have to pump air into the lungs and cause them to cough or they have to add heat to the frozen areas and bring blood back to it. There is pain in the areas where once was peace, but the pain is not bad but rather a life saving pain. God sends his word to our peacefully dying soul and it causes life bringing pain. We should rejoice in our rescue but many fight to remain in their dying state. Many will say the pain is bad, it hurts so they will leave where they are getting healed to go where they are soothed into death. Should the lifeguard or paramedic leave the people to die or continue to try and save those who will be healed? The same question applies to the prophet.

Brother Steve, I'm not a prophet so why is this important to me? God could not speak through the priest because they would not listen, so He had to send special men to deliver His word. Are you so deaf that God needs to send someone to your church or are you a praying pastor, listening evangelist, one who declares "Here am I Lord"? The pastor who is so tied up with counseling that he cannot come to the pulpit and touch a heart that an evangelist can. The pastor who knows there is gossip and confronts it from the pulpit. The pastor who knows there are few who tithe and gives a sermon series on stewardship and tithing. The evangelist who doesn't sing and dance as much as rekindle the fire. God has a message, but He needs men and women who are not hiding under the cloak of conformity but are bravely dancing before the Lord (2 Sam 6:14).

"Correction" is always seen as "Judgment" to those who still love their sin.

The church has often taken its comfort spots in tradition and morals. The traditions allow a routine for the church to perform each Sunday creating an order to the service. When I was in the Air Force I had a priest who timed his sermons to exactly 7 minutes. I thought it quite absurd for a whole hour to be spent for a 7-minute sermon until I sat in a Baptist service and realized between hymns, offering, sacraments, prayer, and altar call there were only about 10 minutes left for a sermon. This standard sequence of service has comfort in it for both the congregation and the pastor. There is nothing wrong with brevity so long as the message is strong and direct, Lincolns Gettysburg address was less than 2 minutes long but was direct and full of message. Other preachers can last an hour every Sunday and sometimes lets the time get away from them. A lengthy sermon touching a point from different angles is not bad either so long as the time is spent on message. But what is the message? Several denominations have their bread and butter in the moral areas. They teach a lot on being good or repenting for being bad but not being holy.

The basis of the message is on the denomination's thoughts on mankind. In the church there are three thoughts on mankind: wicked, errant, victorious. The older churches including the Catholic church believes mankind is wicked in its core and needs to be controlled and punished. The Bible clearly states there is a war within a man between his carnal desires and God. Man comes before God (often through a clergyman) and admits where his control has lacked and what has been the result where he is given a proper punishment. If there is no church, then man will do great evil: like the cannibals on remote islands or the cruel things done in lawless cities like ancient Shanghai. The second group believes man is good at his core but errs and must find forgiveness. This is the group around the time of the Baptist. If you teach them good morals they will endeavor to do right. This is also biblical because Jesus refers to people helping their neighbor. If there is no church then men will come together to create a better community: like certain American Indian tribes or the great minds of Greece. Finally, there is a belief that at the core man is God's image and desires to achieve righteousness but is constrained by this body. That man is fully forgiven of all sins and only needs to love God. This is biblical in some of the writings of Paul. If there is no church then man will serve God through a different name: the Great Spirit of American Indians or the island people who prayed to the sun because they understood that there was something greater than them that caused their lives to be blessed.

There is a difference in being a person with morals and being a moral person. There is a difference in being a person who does holy things and being a holy person. It is not as easy to instill into a person the latter as it is to teach a person to do the former. When I was a boy in a small town one of the first lessons I learned was that my last name stood for something and it was vitally important that I maintain the good name. I was not the Gaskins kid, I was a Gaskins. Every minister knows they are being watched 24/7 to see if they are a man of God or a Godly man. Ministers are not perfect, but they understand that they represent God in all situations and at all times ... but does their congregation know that they do the same? In an effort to not scare off the babes in Christ do you allow seasoned Christians to remain at Sunday school level in their maturity in Christ? A friend of mine used to say he went from ministering to meddling but water never stirred becomes stagnant.

Some pastors point to the number of people who come to the altar each week as proof that their message is working; but are they the same people each week. Some members have a life change that is drastic while others take time, but there should be some movement on a regular basis among your congregation. Elijah did not come to comfort his people, John did not come with the message "relax" and Jesus didn't say "its ok if you just sin a little" … REPENT! REPENT! REPENT! Paul says we do not know we have sin except that the law points it out (Rom 7). Do we whitewash the sermons to the point that the people in the pews do not know they are sinning? Are we satisfied with a congregation that does not cheat on their wives or beat their kids and brings the family to sit on row 6 each week, or do we want to touch lives? Are we the teacher who reads out of the book, or tells a class of spellbound children stories that are not in the book? Some of my favorite teachers were the ones who knew their subject so well they talked about the love for it instead of reading the book. One history teacher talked about the conquistadors leaving in armor, for Oklahoma and returning without their armor and no one has found all those armors: that's not in the history books. Romeo and Juliet is a lot better from the drama teacher than from the book. Is your presentation of the Word of God touching spellbound congregants or are you reading from the book? We can all read scripture, and some are more charismatic than others on interpreting the message, but is your love and pride in your message? I talk about my wife and children with a shine on my face, the same face shows when we talk about Jesus.

CHAPTER FIVE
PREPARING THE WAY

I will go before thee and make the crooked places straight:
I will break in pieces the gates of brass, and cut in sunder
the bars of iron: Isaiah 45:2

THE YOUNG CONCERN themselves with achievements
while the old worry about legacy. Given time to gain
wisdom, most find that the true greatness in life is the lives
you have touched and what they do with that touch. It is
no different within the spirit of Elijah. Moses took a group
of slaves through hard times so Joshua could lead them into
the promise land. Elijah took on Jezebel and her priest of
Baal so Elisha could lead Israel to proper worship. John
brings Israel to repentance so Jesus could give them
forgiveness. These way makers were not perfect men:
Moses had anger issues, Elijah had depression, and John
had doubt. They were willing men who each fulfilled their
mantle from God and they are not zealous that their record

as soul winners, healers, or prophets be glorified: their great mission in life is to "make ready a people" (Luke 1:17).

Moses and Elijah found that they not only had to do their jobs preparing the people, but they also had to prepare their successor. The Bible is clear in God's desire for discipleship (Col 1:27) and this is doubly true within the context of preparing the way for one greater. Through Guiding, Instructing, Focusing and Trusting: we can give those we are mentoring the winning GIFT. Can you imagine if we took everyone in the local school and put them in a large room for study? The kindergartners don't understand Charlotte's Web and the seniors are bored with Cat in the Hat. We would try to teach to a common ground, where the little ones aren't so confused and frustrated that they leave while trying to get the high school students to do more than add and subtract. We would choose to give everyone a book to take home with them and offer classes designed for age groups or interest groups like women, men, college, seniors, or young married couples. It would be chaos. I appreciate the Methodist theory of levels or at least push for the people to attend Sunday school classes at their own level (some couples may have grown at different speeds so they would need to split up here). The thought of our nation using the school system I mentioned earlier is staggeringly scary with only a hand full studying their book at home and a whole nation reading, writing, and doing math at about a 3rd-grade level. How close is that to what American Christians are today? Are we a church like 1st Corinthians 3:1-3 and Hebrews 5:12 where spiritual gifts are plentiful with healings and prophesy abound, yet they are told that they are not mature enough for anything but milk (basic worship)? Would any of your pew sitters go into the church at Corinth and come running out yelling that it's not of God?

We are talking about mentorship and discipleship to churches who can barely get adults involved in Sunday school or Bible study on Sunday or Wednesday nights. In the same time that schools evolved from child labor with only rich kids attending school to a nation where 99 percent are literate and 84.6 percent of children have at least a high school graduation level of education, the church maturity growth has only 55 percent knowing that the Golden Rule is not the 10 Commandments and only 45 percent know the names of the four gospels according to a Pew survey.

In order to make a people ready for a greater glory than the one they have known we must prepare their hearts for a greater repentance than they have known. We cannot wait for the government of laws and judges to teach our members how to obey God's love. The church must stand together on basic things like not killing unborn babies and rape is wrong. There will always be those in the government and in the courts who hate God and his people, but we must turn our attention away from huge churches of spiritual idiots and begin a process of maturing our members who are willing and wanting to grow. Sunday sermon should be a great general time of fellowship and encouragement for repentance and forgiveness ... but growth must happen in the halls and homes of the God-fearing men lest we lose this generation with no one to replace them. I love the old Country song "who's gonna fill their shoes" and I look about the church and ask the same question. When you have a leadership meeting how much snow is on the roofs of your men and women? How many of them has an understudy that they are mentoring? How many of them would have trouble answering a 25-question basic bible quiz like "name the 10 commandments" or "name the 7 churches of Revelation"? Does your music director know the history of "Amazing Grace" or "Because He Lives"? Does your children's ministry leader know why on the third time Jesus asked Peter if he loved him, he told Peter to feed his lambs? If the leadership within your local church isn't ready for a blessing of hungry souls, may I suggest an in-depth study led by the pastor? If you can honestly look at your church and say that your babes are in their classes, your toddlers are in their pews, your elementary development is working, your young adults in Christ are helping with the babes and toddlers, your adults are supervising, and your seasoned Christians are leading the church then Praise God ... you are one of the extreme few.

As I studied the way Jesus trained his disciples, I found that he used the GIFT method too. He didn't take the boys on the first day and prove he was the messiah, then send them out to preach. He walked with them for almost 2 years, having them listen to his teachings, taking the baskets of fish and bread to the people as they multiplied miraculously. They spent evenings together asking questions and being taught in private, they began taking on task for Jesus and sometimes, like when they refused to let the children near him, they were corrected by him. Finally they went out on a buddy system so if one said something incorrectly or got in trouble he would have a friend there to help him, and when they came across something they could not handle like the boy with many demons, they could bring it to Jesus. God understood that training is required before leadership is entrusted. How many talents have gone not used or underutilized because the person could not find a person willing to train them?

Once we have a training system in place, the final step should be an apprenticeship program. There are many areas of ministry including teaching, music, youth, visitation, fellowship, helps, and pastor; many churches have the same person over several of these, but each area is vital to the church along with others that have not been mentioned. Each leader needs to seek an apprentice to train, whether to be their replacement or so they can bless another church with a trained person to do one of these vital ministries. I love a story Pastor Jerry Moore told about a man in his church who would come to him and say I need to go help this church for a while and Pastor would give him leave to go do this work for a year or so, and then welcome him back when he was done. Pastor Moore said the man would ask if he should give back the keys to the church while he was gone, and Pastor would always tell him no because he'd need them again. Are you training up blessings to go help other churches? Especially the larger churches with staff and money for a great training program, imagine the blessing you could be to smaller churches who need a song leader or teacher to fill the gap until God provides one for them. I'll never forget when I first came into the Oologah area as a youth leader for the very small church, Zion Hill, a wonderful man named Thomas Buchanan was leading the youth at the much larger Assembly of God Church in Oologah. He told me that if I needed any equipment or help, to let him know because he understood how much more he had that I might need (he was also at my play that I mentioned earlier to support other leaders in the area). I am so grateful to him and who ever trained him to care for the Christian family as a whole and not just his ministry.

Prepare ye the way for one greater by teaching all that you have and encouraging them to gain more from God. Tent revivals have been around for a long time, but I understand that Oral Roberts lifted them to a new level. He took radio broadcasting and added it to the mix of his tent revival training to create a national ministry. We are not surprised to find that his son Richard was trained to take over, or that Billy Graham has trained his son Franklin, but God did not restrict the Christian faith to only those of a certain bloodline. Speaking of Billy Graham, were you aware that when he graduated high school his sweetheart asked him what school he was going to attend to support their family. When he told her that he was going to Bible school to be a preacher she said there was no money in it and would break off their relationship if he didn't choose a better career. How many obstacles does Satan put in the path to try and stop a preacher including lack of opportunity? Are you seeking the next Elisha out planting a field to call into service?

It has been my experience that the closer I draw unto God the less ego I have. Paul spoke several times about how he was humbled compared to his early years of being a zealot with a badge. John, who was called one of the sons of thunder, was quite meek by the time he received what would become the book of Revelation. Yet many pastors still hold onto their pulpit like it's the last lifeboat on the Titanic. Sunday morning, Sunday evening, Wednesday night, Easter, Christmas, and Groundhog Day: They seldom invite evangelist or guest preachers and they never allow the laity within the church into the pulpit. I do not encourage pastors to neglect their duty to present the Word but I do encourage pastors to allow laity to get some experience in front of a friendly audience under the supervision of a loving pastor.

At A Healing Touch we have a marvelous well-accomplished pianist, Kim Grazier, who is constantly bringing up teens before and after service including having them play and sing a special. They may not be ready for prime time, but they are ready to step out with Kim sitting there encouraging them. In my years of youth ministry, I have met many wonderful adults who have taken one or more under their wing. Mrs. Janice Baker teaching the kids to can vegetables, K.T. Goode teaching them to perform in shadow, and Kathleen Blue teaching them to create thank you cards, and many more. One of the reasons I am so strong on discipleship is because I have worked with teens who are eager to learn, and the future of the church. I utilize them as often as I can from writing a bulletin to taking up offering or working in the clothes closet and feeding the homeless. It gives me great joy when Denise

Epperson taps a teen to help with sacraments or Pastor Moore points directly at the teens and ask if they have a special song. That same spirit of encouragement also needs to be given to the 30 somethings.

Preparing for one greater can include inviting pastors-in-training from the local Bible school to come preach one Sunday. Encourage your members to visit other churches when they have an evangelist or special event. One of my favorite things about attending a church in North Tulsa was the gathering of all the local small churches into a larger church once a month for a Friday night singing. All the pastors would be there along with a couple of grills for food and some serious singing. There was no territorial disputes or pastors trying to "recruit", it was God's people coming together once a month to rejoice.

Have you properly plowed the ground for a harvest to be planted? Are your members ready for a revival? If the church's ship comes in, is the peer built sturdy enough to receive it?

Notes

CHAPTER SIX
TOOLS OF THE TRADE

And ye are complete in him, which is the head of all principality and power. Col 2:10

I HAVE A BAG FULL of tools I carry around when I'm remodeling my home. There are hammers and screwdrivers along with lots of nails and screws. The hammer can put in a screw with enough force, but the screwdriver is much more effective and I don't even want to try getting a nail in with a screwdriver. I have both nails and screws because they both can hold a board in place, but different circumstances call for a different fastener. There's a whole box of other tools and fasteners if these two sets can't do the job. That's how God is with his gifts, he has some that we use a lot like speaking in tongues with interpretation and healing. A word from God through interpretation can soothe the soul but it doesn't do well against a bleeding ulcer and healing can help the ulcer, but it doesn't help me make a decision that's weighing heavily on me. They are not the only tools in God's bag and a person doesn't have to be a prophet to give a prophetic word because God is not restricted to titles.

The spirit of Elijah has three separate parts: uncompromising truth, disturbing healing of the soul, and preparing the way. Separately each of these tools are a powerful force, but combined through and in the spirit of Elijah they create an awesome force for God.

I always enjoy the stories of Paul, but one of my favorites is his walk with Barnabas. Barnabas, like Paul, was a wealthy man with a solid foundation of training, generous and well spoken. He was established among the brethren in Jerusalem and had done some local missionary work but was called to do more. A few years passed since Paul had been a zealot for the synagogue and killing Christians, but the brethren still did not fully trust him. Paul had returned to building houses, but Barnabas knew that Paul had also been called to something more. Barnabas listened to many say it would be foolhardy to take Paul on a mission trip, but Barnabas had faith in God's judgment. The two began traveling and discussing the truth of Jesus the Christ. Paul told him about his wilderness interaction with Jesus and Barnabas told him about his time with Jesus and his disciples. There were some disagreements between them because they were both alpha males, but nothing that could not be resolved. Barnabas was already an established missionary and Paul had much to learn about how to interact with potential Christians in the cities. At some point the teacher stepped back and pushed the student to the front. We find in Acts 14:12 "and they called Barnabas, Jupiter; and Paul, Mercurius (Mercury), because he was the chief speaker." Yet in Acts 14:14 it is declared that both held the office of apostle. What would have happened if Barnabas had not accepted Paul as his companion or tried to keep Paul from attaining the office of apostle? Because they were both apostles, great works were done. Two fantastic tools in God's bag working together against well-established strongholds of the enemy. Doing things that had never been done before in their office of apostle. Where in the bible does it say to use God's power to silence an enemy? They eventually left each other to do their own ministry, but not before opening doors which others would not have had the strength to open. They didn't do it with weak tea truth or appeasing the locals. In Acts 13 & 14 we find them continually upsetting the local Jews. I love in Acts 13:46 when they wax bold and declare to the Jews "... but seeing ye put it from you, and judge yourselves unworthy of everlasting life, lo, we turn to the Gentiles" Does this sound like they were afraid of hurting feelings with God's Word and they cared enough about your soul to make it uncomfortable?

Paul and Barnabas may not have worked under the mantle of the spirit of Elijah, but they certainly used the aspects of the spirit to create a new church throughout the southern part of Europe. If a church or ministry will adopt these into their work, they will find success as well.

There have been many groups that did better than a single person could have done, that may be why God said man is not to live alone (Gen 2:18). Now it is true that God was referring to a marriage to his helpmate, but it is also true that two can often accomplish more than one alone. I once made the comment that my best friend Archiel Spencer Jr. and I were a great team because we would play off each other's ideas. It is quite common for two people to achieve better ideas than working alone. How many pastors today try to be the sole brain trust in their church? They go into their office and pretend that a top-secret meeting is happening? When was the last time the deacons and the pastor went on a retreat to set the course for the church over the next 5 years? It is amazing what God can do with 10 praying leaders in a church concentrating on God's will for their local parish.

In business school we are asked a simple question ... why? Why should I build a new gas station instead of investing in the established one over there? Why should I open a diner instead of helping grow someone else's? The same question is true ... why do I keep this small church with 30 people open instead of joining the bigger church down the road? What do I offer that they cannot get at the other church? What makes me special? God has called the church into being and given it some Godly hearts, but he wants them to work together and accomplish far more than the pastor alone (making house visits, hospital calls, praying with people he meets) can accomplish.

A church full of all age groups serving in their heart's ministry is a wonderful thing. No one saying "been there and done that" like God quit calling you because the government said you were too old to work. No teen whining that they don't know how because they can't get a seasoned individual to teach and train. No Christians complaining because everyone doesn't want to do their heart's ministry. God says He will bless everything we put our hand to, but we have to put our hand to something in order for there to be blessings.

CHAPTER SEVEN

FATHERS TURN TO THEIR CHILDREN

Or what man is there of you, whom if his son ask bread,
will he give him a stone? Matt 7:9

THE SPIRIT OF ELIJAH combines to create three wonderful powers that transform a people. The first one is turning the love of a father or mother toward their children. You may argue that it is a natural thing that does not need to be addressed? I tell you it is neither natural nor in great supply in America.

The natural thing to do is to be selfish. A baby who does not care if you're late for work, going to a nice dinner, or tired. The most natural thing is to look out for yourself: and in America we do just that. We created the concept of latchkey kids to allow both parents to work. We sit the children in front of mind-numbing electronic devices to keep them quiet while we do our thing. I was called weird because I did not let my children watch certain shows that were geared toward children, but taught things I disagreed with: like homosexuality is ok or white people are inherently bad. We call family time sitting around the television quietly watching the same show. We hand our children over to a school that Glenn Beck calls nothing shy of child abuse, where they are taught conformity includes acceptance of sin and not praying in public.

We used to point toward the bad side of town where the girls wore skimpy clothing and were often pregnant early. Today the middle-class girls are wearing short shorts with the word "Juicy" across their bottoms. The local high school says no blankets from home (I never dreamed of taking my blanket to school) because the kids were having sex in the hallway under the blankets. Lest we forget about the new fad is wearing leggings: we used to call them colored pantyhose. What has all this new-found freedom given our children?

The CDC tells us that 1 in 20 kids are addicted to drugs or alcohol and about the same number of girls are pregnant before they graduate high school. Abstinence is considered a myth, but polling has found that about 60% of teens wait until they're 17 before having sex. Drugs and alcohol have been a part of teen life for a long time, but legalizing marijuana does not help keep teens from harming themselves by smoking. There has been a serious attempt to reduce or eliminate teen tobacco use along with a challenge to this new system of vaping, while pushing for the smoking of marijuana. I have heard that the marijuana on the streets today is about 10 times as powerful as it was 40 years ago.

Almost 10% consider their lives so horrible that they cut themselves because the pain brings relief. This was not a major challenge 50 years ago when a child had chores and social attacks were often met with physical altercations. Most teens had a job or worked at home, but today we have more freedom and leisure along with a group of kids that cannot handle a little discomfort.

This inability to handle life challenges like bullying has some differences from years ago, namely when most of us were kids we could walk in the house and stop the bullying and it was usually heard by the kids in a small area then forgotten. Today with social media it follows a kid into their home and hundreds of people from nearby as well as people far away read the attacks. Oologah had a young boy about 12 years old kill himself last year because a full-grown woman in another state was befriending him and then encouraging him to kill himself. This inability to escape the attacks has festered into deep depression and over 5,000 teens attempt suicide every day.

As adults we don't seem to be able to lead by example. According to the CDC over 44,000 commit suicide each year with an additional 1.1 million others attempting to do the same. Almost 3 percent have panic anxiety and almost 8 percent are having severe depression with 16 million being alcohol dependent, 8 million dependent on illicit drugs, and over 2 million having a dependency on both.

The schools tell our children to conform by accepting everyone and not to bully, but they're getting bullied, body shamed, and attacked relentlessly. They turn on television or watch a movie and see teens that are pretty with great bodies being in love while their lives don't match the screen. They come home to parents and siblings wrapped up in their own worlds, who push a distraction in front of the teens and complain about rebellion. I have worked with many teens during my years in ministry and most of them loved me because I did one thing no one else would do ... listen. They have opinions and frustrations they want to share but their peers may think they are stupid, and the adults are too busy, so they bottle everything up. Then they hear or read a catch phrase about "you can be anything", but life teaches them that they can be anything but an interruption.

Women have sacrificed being a mother for being an equal to a man. The primary loss is over 800 abortions every day. We have literally placed our babies on the altar of sacrifice to the idols of convenience and profit. Almost 60 percent of women work outside of the home with three-quarters of them working full time. Women comprise 57 percent of college graduates but are also most likely to get a degree in a non-profit producing major like African American Studies or Pottery. Women continue to be the main employees for food industry and teleservices which are low waged and often late night. This is not to say that women need to be home, barefoot and pregnant, but it is to say that women need to choose careers where they can enjoy their family and study income producing areas. This also means that men need to step up around the house, and not be so insecure as to worry about who brings the most money into the home. My wife earns more than I do largely because I pushed her to achieve the most out of life, she has her master's degree in psychology and works helping the people I've been talking about. I cannot imagine my ego stopping her from becoming the woman she is today. I cannot imagine the lives of those she has helped if I had been so selfish and insecure as to hold her back. We have six children and many teens we have ministered to that love us because we put them first. I have yet to die from doing dishes or folding clothes, and I assure you I am more like John Wayne than Elton John.

We have destroyed the family unit both with government help (no help for dependent children if the father is in the house (1935-96)) and without government help (unwed mothers and couples living together without being married). In the 1970s with the "no-fault divorce" a statistic was thrown out that 50 percent of marriages end in divorce. That number is closer to 30 percent with the second and third being a greater risk. But, throw into that number the group that "co-habitat" and the number increases substantially. The children of broken homes whether with or without a marriage license is over half with a black child having over an 80 percent chance of not having both parents in their home through high school.

So we bought a home to store the stuff we believe we need but never see because we are too busy working for a company that is open 24 hours a day so we can afford the stuff we have purchased, and somewhere in our desire to own everything, we have lost the most precious thing in the home … family.

When the hearts of parents are in Christ the priorities shift. The sanctity of the marriage bed is restored. I'm not suggesting that parents remain in a dangerous marriage for the sake of the children, but children are a precious gifts from God and not inconvenient time stealers. The spirit of Elijah will cause abortion clinics to close down due to lack of business, because husbands and wives won't be having children outside of marriage. Teen girls won't have daddy issues and get with old men to feel love and acceptance. Fathers will encourage their children to achieve success rather than blame them for their own shortcomings. Mothers will fulfill their God-given ability of nurturing their children into healthy wholesome young adults. Children can have nutritious meals with a loving family who wants to discuss their day instead of fast food in front of a television or computer screen where they get life lessons from strangers. As a youth leader for over 30 years, I can tell you the difference in having a strong parent relationship is obvious in a child's attitude and aptitude.

The church will see more parents come see their children in church plays and such. The church will get greater cooperation from children with rising self-esteem from a loving home. As the family unit strengthens, a bond will occur in the pews within the church. The selfish ego will be replaced with a community mind where the church can grow.

Pastors will continue to need to give family counseling because we are still human, but it will be less about infidelity and more about conflicts in personalities. Won't that be nice?

NOTES

CHAPTER EIGHT

CHILDREN TURN TO THEIR FATHERS

Let your father and mother have joy and let her who gave birth to you rejoice. Pro 23:25

THIS POWER OF ELIJAH has two parts, one that is immediately recognized and one that is hidden. The first is the young reaching forth toward their mother and father: the second is the adult children giving respect and care for their elderly parents.

I once saw a man upset as his son ran down the driveway. He looked at me and said it had been just a year earlier they had been best friends, but today it seemed like his son hated him. I explained that one of the growing pains a youth goes through is trying to determine who he is in life. He doesn't know who he will become, but he knows he doesn't want to be who he was: and who he was is a lot like dad. So he rebels, not against the parent but against the old person whom he used to enjoy so he can create a new person. The funny part is that as he goes along, he will find that he has continually found parts of dad to incorporate into the new person, until he becomes older and hopes he has enough of his dad to make it without him.

It is the same with us and God, that we grow up as altar boys who wish to make Jesus happy and become teens with a rebellious heart. We spend the next few years trying to decide what kind of man or woman we are to become: dating, choosing a career, getting married, having a baby, getting drunk and dancing the night away. Then we begin to mature into a parent and before long we are back in church trying to raise a family in God's wisdom until finally we are well seasoned as a person and hope that we represent Jesus well in our life.

Patience is not kind when waiting for a child to make it full circle; each generation believes that the youngsters of today are horrible and will ruin everything. My great grandmother was a young lady during WWI when the wild women liked to dance close to the men. My grandmother was a young lady in WWII when the women began acting too much like a man by working in the factories. My mother was shameful in the 60s twisting around to that rock-n-roll. How could I ever turn out well with those big hair bands influencing me. Today its video games and … ok I must admit that the kids today still listen to my big hair bands, so they're not all bad. But there is one major difference.

I wrote earlier about the shift from farms and small towns to large towns. One of the major drawbacks to this move away from close-knit family towns is a lack of respect for the elders. The elders used to be a relative and your family made sure they were respected. Today the elders are just old people living in the area. The latchkey kid who was not shown nor taught respect cannot find it in their heart to honor the seniors of life … without Jesus.

Even if my father and mother abandon me,

the Lord cares for me. Psalm 27:10

It's easy to love and respect a senior who presents herself as a lady, hair always done and properly dressed. Or the Aunt Bee style lady who just looks like she has a batch of cookies in the oven. The gentleman with his hat on and walking with confidence is easy to respect too. What about the senior that is all bent over or has a sour attitude? The one who has gotten bitter with time and wants respect without giving any. Why would there be bitterness? Because the young person runs past them bumping into them and turning around yelling for them to get out of the way. The con man knowing they don't always think quickly but have a life-savings, stealing it from them with a contract. The government always scaring them by saying that the other side is taking away their money, and the other side saying their account is running out of money. Their children, too busy with a life their parents helped them create, to come visit. They don't want a nursing home because people go there to die. They are lonely and can become bitter. Once gone they become a headstone visited once a year for a while and then forgotten completely.

Does the son who is busy working and raising a family, disrespect his mother by not holding her hand and covering her shoulders with a shawl to keep her warm? Is the daughter who has became the taxi for the family, working, dinner, ball games, ballet, and church, dishonoring her father because she can't make time for him? Are these busy adults any better or worse than the teenager they have raised who do not respect their elders? Should we all live Red Sovine's song "Roses for Mama"?

How devoted does a child have to be to their parent? Many were raised believing they get 18 years then they are on their own. How does that stack up against the responsibility of the child to come back home when their parents reach old age and need help? With parents living long enough to attend their child's retirement party, is it fair to ask an old man to care for his older mother? What if your parents don't know you because of mental illness like Alzheimer's Disease?

My grandpa Gaskins was a well-respected man around Slick Oklahoma but in the latter years his mind wasn't right. Once he got in the pick-up and went down the highway. While he was out driving, he stopped and asked some men standing by a fence if they had seen his cows. The men knew him and that he hadn't had cows in years, so they told him that his sons had got them and pointed him back toward home. Then they called the family and my dad and uncles went out and waved him down as he drove by. That was the end of his having truck keys, and it was the beginning of family taking care of him instead of him taking care of the family. There was no sending him to a home or starving him to death, as I have read where some state is allowing to happen. There was a responsibility by both the children and their spouses, because when you married into the family you became a member of that family.

Today it seems like every person has a "mommy dearest" memory of their childhood because it wasn't perfect. Since when did the child get perfect? A selfish generation has developed out of the generation that demanded love not war and living in a commune. The world of Dr. Spock for children have become the world of Dr. Kevorkian for parents.

This disrespect is what the world would have you see, it is rampant in the areas where God has been removed, like the West Coast and Northeastern area of the United States. There is still many fine young men and women who take the time to hold the door for the elderly, to help them up the stairs, to listen to stories about a time long ago. Many families struggle to keep mom or dad home or have them move in with them. Some have them live with them because they love them so deeply while others can't afford the high cost of a nursing home. Having healthier seniors helps this area very much, my mother is almost 80 and acts younger than I do most of the time.

Where has the church been during the past 50 years while this transition has been in effect? Why is the church so silent on honor and respect? Has it been so muzzled with evening news stories about Jim Bakker's dog house, Jimmy Swaggart's hire a date, Peter Popoff's hearing aid,

Benny Hinn's swishing, pedophile priest, Karan burning preachers, and other things that make the world upset with the church? Which is worse, the way the world shines a light on anyone who tries to give God greatness like the sudden alcoholic and anti-Semitism of Mel Gibson after he made the movie "The Passion of the Christ", or the way preachers savage each other to climb the ladder to a bigger and better church? Are we like the times of Elijah when all the true men of God are either dead or in hiding?

What is the role of the church in teaching the community to fulfill the commandment "Honor thy Father and thy Mother"? Sanctity of life does not only have to do with abortion it also has to do with euthanasia. I have cared for the elderly, including those with dementia, and it is not easy, but every minute of every day is precious to them and to God. There was a man who decided he would say when he died, but every day he would decide the next one was too important to miss until he finally passed away in God's time. Why, because life is special. Why is it that people survive for years in captivity, including POW camps where a person is barely kept alive, why not stop eating and just die ... because life is PRECIOUS. Where there is life there is hope. The world says that these expenses are no longer productive and need to be removed, much like the old movie "Logan's Run". But there is great value in these lives, much wisdom and humor along with a great deal of love to share.

As I stated earlier, being a rebellious teen is part of growing up but being rude about it is bad form. There is no reason a parent should accept their child being rude to others. It is the church's duty to help teach parents how to raise a child. That discipline is not torture or hate but rather it is love that you correct a child, so the state doesn't have to send them to a correctional institute. To teach your child restraint is better than to give them everything so that they value nothing. Hard work begins with chores so they understand that we must often do what we dislike so we can do what we do like. The state's version of this is to threaten the parents with jail if their child disobeys but removes the child if you discipline them; far worse happens in state care (foster) than is allowed by parents. The church needs to know the actual law and teach the parents what is permissible (many DHS workers make up stuff because the people are ignorant). Since when do we release our charges to face the government unarmed (especially the poor) with a prayer but no information or guidance?

The nursing home business is getting rich because families want to pay others rather than slow down or stop their own lives. It is cheaper to send a person on a cruise or stay in a swanky hotel with room service than it is to live in a nursing home. I'm not saying it is easy and for some it is not possible (due to falling and other health reasons), but for many it is just convenience. My wife worked at an inpatient mental facility and she was saddened by the number of parents who put their child into there just so they could have a sitter while they go on vacation. There are several people who drop off their child or have their child go to daycare after school just so they are not bothered during their day. These parents would rather pay a company and enjoy their private time than to be a full-time parent. The children have learned well and now they pay a company to care for the parents so they can enjoy their private time. This needs to stop, and it begins with the pulpit addressing the issue and not worrying about who is being offended.

Again, I say that just because the state legalizes sin does not mean the church has to condone it. If the state outlawed marriage would the church condone couples not being monogamous? There have been many rulers in the last two millenniums who have not been pro-Christian values, but it has not stopped the church from teaching or the congregations from acting in a Christian manner. Somehow the church thinks it is better to ask the state courts to make decisions rather than to accept its role in America. State care for the elderly along with Euthanasia may become legal but it does not have to be condoned by the church. I would not be surprised if the news suddenly started showing stories of chronic pain and dementia patients who have gotten into the weather and died horrible deaths; suddenly there is a law passed to help these poor people through euthanasia (it has already been breached as a byproduct of the opioid situation). Will the church silently allow the state to kill the elderly or hire lawyers so the pastors don't have to offend anyone. This plan has worked so well for the unborn in America.

The world has sped up and given us more free time to have with our family but again, the family seems to be the one thing that has been neglected. The church needs to encourage its members to be as devoted to Christ as they are to their favorite sports team, tv show, and be just as willing to sacrifice their comfort toward shows or people that attack their Christ, like Joy Behar who declared Vice President Pence mentally unstable for believing he hears God during his prayers.

The lovers of God need to make room in their lives for those whom God made custodian over them. They made mistakes and need forgiveness, but for the most part we believe they did what they believed to be best for their children. The beginning of this inclusion is the church cherishing the elderly and finding a place for them and their wisdom in the church: Even the retired want to feel useful.

The lovers of sin will continue to be self-centered and attack everything pure and innocent. But the leaders of the church must be strong and brave as they ask their charges to surrender to God and his plan which is not letting the widows sit at the door of the king for table scraps, but rather sit at the chapel's table to get fed and loved for their value as God's creature. The lovers of sin will try to entice the prodigal son into wasting all that he has but the church must always be prepared to bring him home again.

The fence sitters will justify their situation while the devoted will take the time and effort it takes to earn the money for the nursing home and spend it on doting over their parents. The young adults will set aside the weekend to be a part of the family that loves them so deeply. The father's and mother's will cherish their children and forget to say I told you so and simply ask if they need any help. God made us a family for a reason, and we need to love each other as Christ loves us:

unconditionally and completely.

CHAPTER NINE
PEOPLE TURN TO THEIR GOD

Repent, then, and turn to God, so that your sins may be wiped out, that times of refreshing may come from the Lord. Acts 3:19 (NIV)

THE WAYS OF GOD are always better than the ways of man. Man has managed to take God's perfect way and distort it many times over the centuries: There have been many theocracies over the centuries including The Holy Roman Empire, Byzantine Empire, Spanish Inquisition, Salem Witch Trials, and the only current Christian Theocracy, The Vatican City. Theocracies led by men have all crumbled under the same weight that Jesus found God's temple when he arrived, full of rules to keep people down and poor, while keeping the power in the church. I do not like the way the government has encroached upon the liberties of the church in America, but I am thankful that America has been a place of religious tolerance rather than a theocracy. Having said that, our culture and beliefs have drifted so far from God's word that it is now time for America to repent and return to God.

The time of denominational loyalty is diminishing as is the time for local churches built on generational growth. The culture is fast moving and the traditional ways are appealing for the aging generations, but not for the microwave society that currently exist. Many of the current churches that are expanding do so through modern pathways, just as the church changed from big organs to a piano with a band of drums and guitars. The Sunday best clothing required for entry has been replaced with the comfortable and relatively conservative clothing including jeans, and t-shirts. Some believe this change in attire is disrespectful to God's house, but others note that many who felt disenfranchised now feel welcome and become members.

Why do people go to church? I will always remember what President Obama said when it was discovered that his pastor was teaching politically incorrect messages, "I didn't know". He had sat through the sermons but did not know what was said. He is like many who attend church; there to shake hands and be seen but not to worship the Lord. With the change in attitude many no longer care if they are seen as a member of a certain church or even a respectable member of society.

The mega-church has hundreds on staff using every way to reach people with their message, but how many are teaching Christ and how many are selling Christ. There are two distinct and opposite sets of verses in the Bible and many teach one and avoid the other, this is not new but the one chosen to teach has changed. One set is popular today and it is based upon Luke 11:9 " ... ask and it shall be given you ..." along with Luke 6:38 "give and it shall be given unto you; good measure, pressed down, and shaken together, and running over ..." but this ATM Jesus is not free stuff with no strings attached. The other set that was taught by what were known as fire and brimstone preachers was based on Mark 10:21 "... take up thy cross and follow me" along with Romans 6:23 "For the wages of sin is death; but the gift of God is eternal life through Jesus Christ our Lord". The old ways were filled with fear of punishment, but the new ways are filled with unending free stuff from a God who doesn't require a circumcised heart. I have lived long enough to see greedy churches fall and members promised the world from God realize their rainbow has no pot of gold, only a shovel and a plow to earn a living. God can and will bless those who believe but he will not be someone's errand boy to come and go with presents.

There is to be a massive shaking down of the church just as it has been happening for the last 40 years. First the great televangelist of the 80s promised all sorts of things to pay for television time and a lifestyle, but eventually the mail in offerings and the local church did not keep up with demand or they determined themselves greater than the God they preached about and fell. The televangelist always find a pattern to follow, get charismatic teachings, get an audience, expand to regional or national, begin cutting teachings short so you can either hock your wares (books, tapes, live conference, Saul and Peter salt & pepper shakers, etc) to make more money or introduce others to your audience in an interview rather than surrender your pulpit for a viewing. Soon the audience reduces because they're not getting what was promised and soon they are replaced with someone new; but the disappointed follower doesn't go to a local church they simply stop believing in Jesus. Romans 2:24 "For, as it is written, "the name of God is blasphemed among the Gentiles because of you."" Is it any less true that the name of Jesus is blasphemed among the heathens because of the Christians?

We cannot complain about the heathens acting in a heathen way. It is no surprise that the heathens attack the cross when the church will not stand up for it. The heathens give bundles of money to the ACLU to attack Christians, but the church does not support the ACLJ. We can no longer have a nativity scene in town square, prayer before a football game, say the name of Jesus during high school valedictorian speech (though the judge's rule was unconstitutional), have state money to fix historic churches, use state money to help finance food and clothing for the homeless ... but if you want to kill unborn babies you can get millions from the state. Heathens will not protect the church and the state is full of heathens. It does not take long to look at the legislation and court decisions to know that God is not a priority in the congress, federal courts, bureaucracy, education systems, news or entertainment. When was the last time a star came out attacking the church and the members actually suffered through not seeing one of their shows or movies? Tim Tebow is attacked for kneeling for prayer on football field, but we manage to abstain from football when the kneeling is applauded during the national anthem. Megan Kelly can be fired for asking what is wrong with blackface, but Joy Behar can say the Vice President has a mental illness because he believes he hears from God when he prays, and the church stays silent as a lamb being led to slaughter. Can we not miss the latest movie by a Christian hating star or vote based on Christ rather than party? There was a time when non-Christians could not stay in business if they attacked the church, today the church is afraid it will upset the

Christians if it attacks the non-Christians. It is the church that teaches morals not the state. It is obvious that the state is set on a course that is not toward a Christian nation, but this is still a nation of people and the church's influence over the people can correct the course.

I have declared to both Jews and Greeks that they must turn to God in repentance and have faith in our Lord Jesus. Acts 20:21 (NIV)

There are two men with distinctly different approaches to following God's call: The man who asked Jesus to allow him to bury his father (Matt 8:21) and Elisha who burned his plow (1 Kings 19:21). Elisha was not gung-ho to leave his family in a bind of not having equipment to work their fields, in fact he asked Elijah to give him time to say goodbye to his parents and Elijah said to go ahead and enjoy your family life but miss the call of God (1 Kings 19:20). Both men were called and both men wanted to wait until their family had passed and their prime productive time had waned to begin the gentler life of spreading God's word. Their reaction is quite different when called on their procrastination: Elisha burned his plow and sacrificed his oxen because he wanted God to know he would have nothing to tempt him to return, while the man Jesus called did not get on the boat with Jesus (Matt 8:22). How many are in the church waiting until they are done with their life before they are willing to give their life to God. The vast majority of pastors in America are over 40 (about 6 out of 7), is that due to resilience of pastors over the years (most do not last over 5 years) or the reluctance of youth to commit. Teens are renowned for their desire to be involved, many high schools and colleges thrive on the volunteer spirit of the young. If you want to march on town hall, get the teens active passing out flyers and making banners, If you want to save the squirrels or build the world's largest taco … get the teens to help, because most of the adults have become accustomed to a routine and don't want to get involved in things. So why is it that church camps for teens and college kids are swamped with volunteers to be missionaries but the church can't convert that into pastors, evangelist, and missionaries?

One reason people don't go to church is that they are not asked. Dr. Jon Wakefield, pastor of Harvest Church in Jenks Oklahoma, did his thesis on how to retain visitors and he makes it a point to make sure each visitor is invited back and follow up is sent. The same is true on why people are not active in their church or why they leave a church. How many pew sitters would be willing to be ushers or greeters if they were simply asked? A person doesn't have to know every verse to smile and open the door for people. Once involved in the church, people have a greater tendency to come regularly and feel needed instead of a guest who no one would notice if they simply stop coming. A general statement to the entire congregation does not work as well as a few seconds during a handshake to say "brother could you help with offering/communion today" or "sister could you help collect visitor cards this morning." The ministry of helps is a great place to recruit among your congregation.

As a youth minister I made it a point to have my teens serving as ushers and greeters during the service: to learn that service goes with Christianity.

According to churchleaders.com less than 20 percent of Americans attend church regularly. The number of people who believe in God is slightly lower than 20 years ago, except among the high school/college students who have an increased number who do not believe in any organized religion. This is not new, while they may be ready to join a movement they are not always ready to agree with their parents about things, including religion. In time each generation will return to where their children and grandchildren need to be. Always remember there is a time between child and when he is old.

Train up a child in the way he should go: and when he is old, he will not depart from it. **Proverbs 22:6**

One of the major issues with the moral majority is comfort. We have some Hollywood actors attack Christianity and the Christians refuse to miss their movie or television show. The President says we are not a Christian nation and the church sits quietly hoping to be defended by … I give up … who? When the follower asked to follow Jesus in Matthew 8:19 & 20 Jesus said come on but know that most of the time I sleep under the stars. I will teach you great things, give you lots of love, allow you to do great miracles … but we won't be staying the night in luxury homes and eating at the best tables. He, like the other follower, did not get in the boat with Jesus. There was a time when the country feared the religious people. The famous letter by Thomas Jefferson where he states that there should be a hedge between the state and the church, the same letter that the courts use to say separation of church and state but insist on having the church out of the state instead of the state out of the church, was written because pastors held such sway over their congregation that Jefferson needed their support to be president. Today, if a preacher speaks on anything political, they are threatened with losing their 501(c)3 status (making their donations tax deductible). If they have scared the pastors into silence with tax money, how hard will it be to scare them into surrendering a copy of their sermon (the courts in Texas have already ordered it once). The Muslims are feared because they will burn down your house and kill people (fire in January 2018 at St. Catherine University to protest President Trump), the gay group with too many letters to remember will march and destroy property (1992 Academy Awards), the liberals destroy Berkley University when a conservative is invited to speak in 2017, and other groups that are feared by both politicians and the media. Where is the fear of the huge number of Christians who are attacked regularly but the attacks are not condemned? The show "God Friended Me" recently took the storyline to shame Christians who do not accept gays but the show is still just as popular as before. It's hard to watch a show without seeing a gay couple kiss or a girl to get almost naked for no apparent reason, Luke Cage is about a black superhero who is bulletproof and extra strong when suddenly he must take some new girlfriend to his apartment and get almost naked with her ... why? Because the moral majority will not turn off the television and refuse to watch ... they're more concerned about pleasure and comfort than standing up and demanding respect. If Jesus came to the church today and demanded that those who follow him to only watch shows that do not cuss or get naked or glorify any other form of sin (gay, theft, murder, adultery, etc), how many would turn away from Christ. Jesus is not the Lord of leisure, he is the King who says take up thy cross and follow me ... die to yourself and be transformed. How many will refuse to get in the boat with Jesus if they have to surrender their R-rated viewing habits? The answer is not enough, and that keeps those in charge of creating shows and movies ignoring them.

The church did not become weak suddenly; it has taken decades of erosion and small surrenders. I don't know who wrote the story but it goes like this:

A Stranger in the House

A few months before I was born, my dad met a stranger who was new to our small Tennessee town. From the beginning, Dad was fascinated with this enchanting newcomer, and soon invited him to live with our family. The stranger was quickly accepted and was around to welcome me into the world a few months later. As I grew up I never questioned his place in our family. Mom taught me to love the Word of God. Dad taught me to obey it. But the stranger was our storyteller. He could weave the most fascinating tales. Adventures, mysteries and comedies were daily conversations. He could hold our whole family spellbound for hours each evening. He was like a friend to the whole family. He took Dad, Bill and me to our first major league baseball game. He was always encouraging us to see the movies and he even made arrangements to introduce us to several movie stars. The stranger was an incessant talker. Dad didn't seem to mind, but sometimes Mom would quietly get up - while the rest of us were enthralled with one of his stories of faraway places - and go to her room to read her Bible and pray. I wonder now if she ever prayed that the stranger would leave. You see, my dad ruled our household with certain moral convictions. But this stranger never felt an obligation to honor them. Profanity, for example, was not allowed in our house - not from us, from our friends, or adults. Our longtime visitor, however, used occasional four-letter words that burned my ears and made Dad squirm. To my knowledge the stranger was never confronted. My dad was a teetotaler who didn't permit alcohol in his home - not even for cooking. But the stranger felt he needed exposure and enlightened us to other ways of life. He offered us beer and other alcoholic beverages often. He made cigarettes look tasty, cigars manly, and pipes distinguished. He talked freely (much too freely) about sex. His comments were sometimes blatant, sometimes suggestive, and generally embarrassing. I know now that my early concepts of the man/woman relationship were influenced by the stranger. As I look back, I believe it was the grace of God that the stranger did not influence us more. Time after time he opposed the values of my parents.

Yet he was seldom rebuked and never asked to leave. More than thirty years have passed since the stranger moved in with the young family on Morningside Drive. But if I were to walk into my parents' den today, you would still see him sitting over in a corner, waiting for someone to listen to him talk and watch him draw his pictures. His name? We always called him TV.

That is a great story and who ever originally wrote it, thank you.

CHAPTER TEN

SMALL BUT STRONG

So that you may live a life worthy of the Lord and please him in every way: bearing fruit in every good work, growing in the knowledge of God.
Colossians 1:10 (NIV)

THE CHURCH IS GOING to be reduced from the important social gathering to the diligent servants of God.

The revival that has been prayed for by so many will accomplish the separation of the devout from the deva, the warrior from the wisher, and the hardened from the hardly. If you have seen a person taken by the Spirit and begin to run with their friend who wants to pretend as he runs around the church ... you understand the difference. One is led by God to run full blast around a corner that his body cannot make but God's will has him do; the other is slowing down, running into walls and worn out physically.

Are you ready for a time when God touches the church in a mighty way to prepare her for the coming attacks? Are your people in the pews ready to be hardened for battle? Are the pastors ready to have a move where many will leave, but the remnant will be fully devoted to Christ? A prayer for the spirit of Elijah is a prayer for persecution that creates victory. David did not hide in the caves because the shepherd life was too boring; he was there because God had to make a king out of him. Are you ready to have a church filled with kings? Bishop T. D. Jakes likes to say that many want what he has but they don't want to pay the price he has paid to get there. Steve Harvey says his children were not there when he was homeless, but they enjoy the life he can now provide for them. Are you ready to speak fire from the pulpit?

And not only so, but we glorify in tribulation also; knowing that tribulation worketh patience.

Romans 5:3

The spirit of Elijah is needed in America and throughout the world. We desperately need a solid foundation of truth that is uncompromising; not willing to be watered down with nuances but is strong in God's word ... bold. I once started to teach on the full armor of God but only got to the belt of truth because it is so fundamental to everything else. Truth is what holds the rest of the armor together. Truth is the center of all that God has for us. Truth is so important that if there is any aspect to the Word of God that is not truth all that is God's word becomes undone; that is why so many have tried desperately to find one small part inaccurate in the Bible. The reason the world hates Christians is not because we pray or feed the hungry, it's because we bring the truth to which their actions and intent must be measured, and the world is so often found wanting but God's word is always perfect. The statement, if you cannot find fault in the message, attack the messenger, is the reason so many pastors are attacked by other preachers who are more interested in social issues than God's word. Pastors are simply redeemed sinners who God has called to proclaim the perfect truth spoken by a perfect God. Jesus says "fear not" but it is fear of loss that causes the pulpit to add water to God's word that the babies can drink it instead of growing the babies up to the point that their stomachs can handle it. God said that the truth shall set us free not some milky white flavorless substitute that won't offend anyone. My prayer for every preacher who is reading this book is that they will boldly proclaim God's precious truth.

So that we may boldly say, the Lord is my helper,
and I will not fear what man shall do unto me.
Hebrews 13:6

It always amazes me, the men and women that God has called into service. A ruddy shepherd, a fallen prince, a murderous zealot, a bunch of fishermen, a coward thrashing his wheat in a cave, an old woman with a sick boy, some prostitutes, and lest we forget a man who took his brothers birthright with a bowl of soup and stole the blessing by fooling his father. This is not the family tree of a king but more like the family tree of the manager at the trailer park. This is who God has chosen to be his instruments. Instead of calling them "The Usual Suspects" we can call them "The Willing". It is a wonderful thing to be called by God into service, but when looking for our laity volunteers, are we too quick to discount the David's when we look for a Saul? We are not God, knowing the heart and the future, but we do need to spend more time being like the wonderful Christian in the song "Hold My Mule" by Shirley Caesar. God does give great gifts to some of the most unusual people, but he is also careful upon who to place a mantle.

Some of you want to balk at this and remind me that God is not a respecter of persons (Rom 2:11), but I must remind you of the other side of that coin:

To whom much is given, much is required (Luke 12:48). Can you imagine if God gave every Christian the power of Elijah? One would be mad and calling down a drought while the other would be proud and calling for the death of an army, meanwhile another would be giving granny a never empty pot of oil. True chaos would come with giving immature Christians too much power.

And the Lord came, and stood, and called as at other times, Samuel, Samuel. Then Samuel answered, speak; for thy servant heareth.

1Samuel 3:10

What are the criteria for being allowed to wield the power of Elijah? It's all in the heart! John the Baptist was not proud, he only wanted to serve God and bring the people to him. Elijah said it best when he declared "I have been jealous for the Lord" in 1 King 19:10. God is no fool that he should give a great power to a child. As a parent I would never look at my 3-year-old and hand him a pistol, or have you seen what transpires when a young, rich and spoiled ruler takes over a country? If we are wise enough to reserve great power for those mature enough to handle great responsibly, do you not believe God to be as wise as us? We may desperately need the spirit and power of Elijah today, just as the children of Israel desperately needed a deliverer for centuries before Moses arrived. Does that mean we should not operate in the spirit of Elijah and prepare a people for the power that is so needed? Glenn Beck was speaking on the radio the other day and made the observation that we do not fight to be a generous nation, we, the people, are generous and the movement will create a generous nation. The same with the church. If we want to be a strong, repentant, glorious church working in all the manifestations and gifts that God has for us we cannot whine or want to be … we must walk as though God has given us the church we want as individual churches and Christian, be jealous for the Lord, then the church will become exactly what the power of Elijah is all about.

May God bless you and yours today

and throughout the forthcoming time of

growing from glory to glory. AMEN

Elijah Power

BONUS

IS YOUR CHURCH FOR SALE?

IT'S SUNDAY MORNING AND THE CHURCH IS
FULL of men in their suits and women wearing their
best hats. The choir sings and the offering is taken.
The pastor steps up to the pulpit like a captain of the
ship and begins to lay out his sermon. The crowd
sits in silent respect as he continues until five
minutes before noon, where he stops and gives the
altar call with the piano playing *"Just As I Am"*.
Across town another church is preparing to let out
their people, they're in blue jeans and a nice shirt,
they're not as silent during the sermon, and the
pastor is happy to have the amen crew today.
Everyone shakes hands and goes to the diner for
lunch as the pastor returns to his office to greet the
unhappy people. The songs were too old or we
need more hymns; the sermon was too long or
needed more fire in the belly, how dare you preach
on tithes and offerings (this is twice this year). Once

that group is done, the church leaders are ready to come in and they shut the door. They have complaints about the building, ministry, budget, and lack of volunteers. Did I mention that the pastor actually had a sermon on the importance of giving back to God and how God rewards a happy giver? This sermon is cheered by some who want more budget, and it is frowned upon by those who have been under a pastor who beat that drum constantly until the church got the reputation of being money hungry. Some say that politics is no place for an honorable man, but they've never examined church politics or they'd gladly move to Washington DC.

This is about one aspect of church politics that intertwines with national politics. This is about certain people who either hate the church and want to see it fall, or are pro-church but more interested in social change than following the Bible. These people have learned how to "interpret" the Bible in a way that suits their desires for the church to become "woke". They won't do it from the pulpit because there would be a backlash in the conservative church. If they can get into the pastor's office as an important member of the church, they can control the church through him. If they can't get their agenda preached, they can deter the pastor from preaching against their agenda: whether its abortion, gay rights, antisemitism, racial inequality, or all religions are the same god.

Is your church for sale? How big a check does it take to be put on the board of deacons? How vetted are your deacons and church leaders? The entrance of wolves in sheep's clothing is nothing new within the church, it goes back to the very beginning of the church. Jesus himself said that he sends us out as sheep among wolves, but then he tells us to be wise as serpents and gentle as a dove.(Matt 10:16) After the ascension of Jesus the disciples found the wolves were truly merciless in their attacks. This brought Paul to write that grievous wolves would attack and not spare the flock, but worse that men would rise up among the members and leaders to draw members away by speaking perverse things.(Acts 20:29-30) Peter told us that there will be false teachers bringing forth damnable heresy (as opposed to differing of opinion) even to the point of denying Jesus the Christ. (2Pet 2:1)

The initial church was small and could easily be governed by a hand full of ministers, if a minister or member started presenting a false doctrine it could be dealt with quickly. A church under persecution doesn't want to be big or have too many people who can tell where too many churches are located. Around the second century the church went from a group of small churches into a group large enough to need organized. This was still dangerous because the government was still after Christians, but there was a need for consistency in the belief. First the bishop of a city would govern the churches in his city and the surrounding towns and villages. Soon there was a need for someone to govern the bishops in a certain area like a region or a country. By the time the government slowed down on the persecution of the church and stopped using Christians for Roman candles (burning them alive on street corners) or lion food, it looked much better for the church, but the leader of the church often found himself exiled by Emperor Maxentius. Administrating over a few churches isn't much power and only takes a little of your time but being a bishop over bishops is a full-time job and has a lot of power. When Constantine the Great recognized the church (313 AD) and declared the empire a Christian place there was a real opportunity for corruption. Power struggles begin with alignments and soon there is a fight between the two great capital cities: Rome and Constantinople. The bishop of Rome wants to be the bishop of God, he is to be declared supreme pontiff or Pope. This is after a large battle within the church that eventually has Rome in charge of the European church that renames itself universal or Catholic and Constantinople in charge of the Asian church that becomes known as the Eastern Orthodox Church.

One man has the authority to set rules about the church and is able to grant favors and allow whom he desires into his inner circle. He is supposed to be a man chosen by God after much prayer, but seeking power is a corrupt sport and making promises of who will be in the inner circle or gets the plum positions soon takes control of the process. One of the first rules that is established is that a priest must be celibate. This is interesting since the Roman church says they follow Peter, who was a married man with children. This does work out great for the church: Noblemen have more than one son but only one can take the crown, they usually have one that will not make a military leader but needs to have a prestigious position that the church can offer. Since the son cannot marry and takes a vow of poverty, he will not need an inheritance but the church needs a donation to bring him to such a prestigious position and that unneeded inheritance will just about cover it. Got a wife or daughter that is unruly but needs a respectable reason for her absence, she can study with the nuns for a generous donation.

Passing rapidly from a condition of distress and persecution to the summit of prosperity and prestige, the church degenerates rapidly from purity to corrupt and forfeits the respect. Noblemen who are used to abusing servants are now in charge of areas of the church where they have no desire to serve God but only to gain personal pleasure. The bishop may have taken a vow of poverty but that hasn't stopped him from living a luxurious lifestyle with a large posh church office filled with servants, an ostentatious robe, feasting on the very best foods and wines. The people of the church have no safety from the abuse because the governing body is friends with the father of the abusive bishop, and if a priest objects he is quickly exiled from the area by both the church and the state. In many areas the bishop has used his influence to become the governing body which is considered a great thing in the church because it means there will be no resistance to church growth. Over time a few new rules were added like fish on Fridays because the church owns the fish market and needs to be more prosperous.

Two of the great non-biblical things that occurred early in the church were 1.)Europeanization of Jesus and 2. Adding the philosophy of yin-yang into the church doctrine. Yin-yang is an Eastern philosophy that says in every bad there is a bit of good and in every good there is a bit of bad, and the two will balance each other. In the church we don't describe it as yin yang: we say that if we are going through a bad time it is because we are about to receive a good blessing. The more hardship we endure the greater the blessing that is on its way. No where in the Bible does it say anything like this, but it is a common belief among church people. I apologize for forgetting which Pope studied in Asia and brought this into the church, but it is well rooted. This corruption has been joined by a much more recent adage of "do your best and God will do the rest" or as Okies like to say "you do your part and God will do his". Maybe this will sound more familiar "God helps those who help themselves" (Ben Franklin's Poor Richard's Almanac in 1757) which could be derived from 2 Thessalonians 3:10 where Paul writes "If anyone will not work, neither let him eat." As for Yin-Yang theory, the Bible says in Galatians 5:17 that "For the flesh desires what is contrary to the Spirit, and the Spirit what is contrary to the flesh. They are in conflict with each other, so that you are not to do whatever you want."(NIV) There is no place for balance between the two, you either resist the body and grow from glory to glory or you submit to the flesh and remain on spiritual milk.

The second step had to do with dominance of the Roman Catholic church. They took away the symbol of the empty tomb or the rolled away stone and put Jesus back on the cross. It is true that the death of Jesus is important, but it's through his resurrection that we find salvation. Without his resurrection he is only another wise man or prophet, but because of his defeating death, hell, and the grave he is proven to be divine. Many believe in Jesus like the belief in Aesop's fables: great moral lessons to help in life. 1 Corinthians 1:23 says "but we teach Christ crucified: a stumbling block to Jews and foolishness to gentile." And through this teaching the church went from an offshoot of the Jewish religion to a persecutor of the Jews. The Eastern Orthodox Church owned the Holy Land, so the Roman Catholic Church needed to make Jesus look more like them and less like the Jews whom they were teaching people to hate. The beard was the first thing to change, no longer thick and woolly it now became thin and straight with the cheeks bare. The hair followed suit, becoming straight and long to go with the nose that was no longer long. Blue eyes and bleached skin made a complete European upon the cross for Christians to lament while blaming the Jews for putting him there.

By the time Martin Luther joins a group of disgruntled Christians to protest the Catholic Church and call themselves Protestants, the rules and regulations of a simple faith have become volumes of study material. There is a story I heard about the reason Martin Luther changed his mind from being a loyal Catholic professor to being a leader of the Protestant rebellion. Martin Luther was in the library which was like today's Christian bookstore in that all the greats and many of the others had written books about some aspect of the Bible for clarity and understanding. He was thumbing through these volumes of understandings when he came upon a book he had never read. After reading it he decided that the Catholic Church had some major issues with God's word: The book was Romans written by Paul in the New Testament.

It is good to share your understandings just like I am doing here, but never allow other's opinions to replace God's word.

In my more than 50 years on this earth I have seen a lot of changes in the church. When I was a boy people wore their Sunday best and the pastor was put on a very high pedestal, it was an honor to have him join your family for lunch. In the 80s the faith people started building churches and invited people who didn't wear suits and dresses. The music was loud, and the messages were strictly promises of faith-filled acts of power and might, from a preacher who claimed to be nothing special.

The faith people loved to take a truth and run without ever digging deep into the Bible to find out the whole story (headline Christians). For instance, God is love and since I believe love is acceptance then God is accepting everything, or we can pick up serpents which has led to a lot of churches I don't enter (me and Mr. No Shoulders don't share a building). It also brought in a lot of con men because there was a large group of naive people with money looking for an experience.

When I was a boy, I was shot in the eye and it partially blinded me. This evangelist in the 80s was preaching healing and how God could and would clear every problem from growing back limbs and making lame people get out of their wheelchairs and walk to healing the deaf and giving sight to the blind. I'm 18 and tired of being blind in the corner of my right eye so I go up for healing. He takes a look at this 6-foot 200-pound kid and says I don't need to know what your problem is, I can see it:

you've got one leg shorter than the other. It was news to me, but he had me sit in a chair and put my feet together, wow it was a good inch different. He prayed and pulled my heel to make both legs the same length. I was so impressed, right up until I was working the midway at the fair and one of the carnies said let me show you a trick. I'm not saying that all faith healers are fake but I am saying that a group of Christians who are running around being the next Peter without taking the years of study, can end up like them boys who cast out demons in the name of Jesus whom Paul speak of. The demon said I know and fear Jesus, I know who Paul is and fear him for his faith in Jesus, but you're just a parrot repeating what you don't understand so I'm just gonna whoop you real good (that's Okie paraphrasing of Acts 19).

Today denominational loyalty is barely kept, and most people couldn't tell you the difference between the different churches, they go to hear the preacher they like, and if he says something they don't like then they will find another church. The sanctity of the chapel is treated as pure as the sanctity of marriage and the sanctity of life.

Speaking of sanctity of things, let's talk about a destruction of a wholesome organization. My son was working on his Eagle Scout when a group of social warriors bought themselves important positions on the Boy Scouts of America's board. They had a young man file to be openly gay in their organization. The group supported him but wanted to make it appear that it was not their fault that the rules changed so they took it to court with full belief that the boy would win. The courts failed them by agreeing that as a private group the BSA could adopt rules prohibiting openly gay boys. Initially the media was supporting the long traditions of the BSA and how inappropriate it would be for camping trips and other activities. Then the board, led by AT&T began attacking itself as homophobic and calling for a change in the rules. The media quickly switched sides and began seeking extreme idiots on the other side. They found people screaming about rapes in tents which common sense said would be rare. The challenge is that the model of the BSA is emulation, the young boys imitate the older boys causing the older boys to be great in the eyes of the younger boys. The scouts build upon that bond to get the younger boys to strive to advance while giving the older boys leadership positions so they can work with the younger boys while they strive to accomplish what the eldest boys (the troop leaders) have achieved. It has worked for over 100 years. Now, the young boy age 12 who is trying to figure out hormones and why that red-headed girl he's been playing tag with is looking prettier and making him want to sit with her, sits down next to the great 17-year-old troop leader whom he is supposed to be emulating and hears how it's good to like boys too. Remember that gays cannot procreate so they must propagate. In the last few years the slippery slope has achieved getting gay scouts under 18 followed by gay leaders over 18 who are now the men who take your 11 - 17-year-old son (and now daughter) out camping with the idea that they should emulate him. They said their reason was to make a more inclusive group, but the Camp Fire Organization already had both boys and girls with acceptance of gays, it just needs money for better public relations because right now it's just an after-school group like 4H. So if they are honest, then why not build up the Camp Fire Organization instead of attacking the honorable Christian organization called Boy Scouts of America?

So it worked, not from the outside but buying your way into the leadership. When the Southern Baptist convention said that they agree with the Bible about women obeying their husbands, it was attacked but to no avail. When the pastor is Florida said he would burn the Koran, and he was beset upon by the federal government until he agreed to stop so he wouldn't go to jail (what crime was he committing?). Lawyers (most lawmakers are lawyers) and judges have long been known to not hold deep religious views while politicians have often claimed religious beliefs to convince their constituents that they have morals and are ethical. For a group of people claiming to be Christians at election time, they sure don't act like it when writing and passing laws. The pastors are threatened if they speak for or against a politician even though the early nation received most of its political opinion at the church. The reason Thomas Jefferson wrote the famous letter about separation of church and state was to convince preachers to encourage their flocks to vote for him.

So what does this have to do with your church? EVERYTHING! Most churches and almost every church over 200 people that I know has a board of deacons appointed by the deacons who were there before them. They are supposed to be the governing body that protects the church, hires the pastor or when necessary fires the pastor. Preachers come and go but the reputation of the church last forever. In theory the deacons would pray before appointing a new deacon, like the disciples did before replacing Judas. In truth it usually goes to a family member of a current deacon or to a friend of the pastor. Sometimes it goes to a new member that is influential like a lawyer or a city council member (this serves both the prestige of the church and the validation of the politician as moral). Quite often the biggest contributors will be sitting on this board governing how the money is spent. So some dentist, doctor, lawyer, politician, or other professional with deep pockets from a liberal school who believes the church is homophobic, non-accepting of the LGBQ (and more letters) agenda, speaking out against abortion, won't admit climate change is man-made, and is totally intolerant and must be stopped ... joins the church and gives generously while asking to be a deacon. There is no test to see how much Biblical knowledge and understanding, in fact many deacons admit to having little Biblical understanding, but they don't need to because they are not teaching or preaching but rather they are handling administration and money. So now the anti-Christian anti-church social warrior is in charge of the mission money and more importantly is on the board that the pastor must keep happy to maintain his job. Sermon on husbands being the head of the house ... GONE. Sermons on homosexuality being a sin ... GONE. Sermons on sanctity of life and abortion being evil. GONE. Sermons wanting to delve into the political attacks on the church will get a swift rebuke by the deacon with a threat of loss of job, and if the other deacons don't like it, they can count his check GONE. Usually they are quietly yelling in the pastor's office or at the council meetings, refusing funds for Christian organizations like American Family Association because they are anti-gay marriage and anti-abortion. The power of the purse is very strong, and if you can get enough board members across the country, you can do things like force Doctors Without Borders to agree to do abortions or go bankrupt. Others use embarrassment to deter pastors, like standing in the middle of a sermon and demanding clarity if the pastor references a certain flag or organization. This is not for better understanding; it is to humiliate the pastor and force silence on the subject with the assurance that as a deacon and a donor they will be exempt from backlash from the pastor and the board.

IS YOUR CHURCH FOR SALE? Sounds harsh and silly but it is all too true in today's church environment. Is your pastor willing to sacrifice his position to preach against sin or will he be intimidated into just putting out a list of "moral" stories? Will you deacons be willing to lose money and influence to protect the pastor and the church from abandoning organizations that fight the good fight against sinful activities that are popular amongst the television personalities? Will the conservative church go the way of the Boy Scouts of America? Will people still find Jesus within your walls or will they find a moral lesson on forgiveness and acceptance?

Elijah Power

THANK YOU!

I want to thank my family for putting up with me (I do seesaw a lot), especially my wife who has been my rock and encourager. Thank you to my mom Kathleen and my sister Stephanie for their love and patience. Thank you to my pastor who has read through my writings and given constructive criticism.

Thank you to my back cover and bio writer: E. Danielle Butler of Tucker GA aka Evydani from Fiverr.

Thank you to my book cover designer Ericgraphic07 from Fiverr.

Thank you to all the countless people on the Internet who have websites, blogs, or videos that I used in learning how to make and publish a book.

GAIN: COMING SOON

Genesis Series Book 1: Beginnings

Beginnings is currently being written and should be published by Spring 2020. This book is an exciting book to write because it goes from pre-creation, Lucifer's rebellion war, creation, fall of man, Cain's betrayal, marriage, and linage, and Noah's flood. Written in a news article style that is set for eighth grade readers with adult information.

Luke Series Book 1: Birth

Birth is in outline stage and should be published by Fall of 2020. This book will cover God's choice of Mary and Joseph, Birth of John the Baptist, and Birth of Jesus. This book you bought is started out as a few pages to clarify what John the Baptist received in the womb but turned into its own book. I look forward to seeing what all God will reveal in this book.

12 Tribes

This special book is also in outline stage and should be published by Fall of 2020. There were 12 sons and 13 tribes because Joseph's tribe was divided between his two sons. Each time that God references them he calls out 12 and places them in an order to where the meaning of the names has a statement about the situation they are in.

Reverends Steve & Mary Gaskins

Author Steve Gaskins is a licensed minister and veteran. He served as a chapel manager for the U.S. Air Force and has served in various ministry roles from soundboard operator to greeter. In addition to the ministry of helps, Steve has worked with teens for nearly three decades. An ongoing student of the Word, Steve began his writing journey after an in-depth, five-year Bible study. It was during this time that he realized that there is a gap between new or young Christians in Sunday School and the teaching and training available to the maturing Christian. Since then, Steve has written with the goal of assisting others in growing from whatever stage of relationship they are in with Christ. Steve's ministry outreach includes books, skits, and plays. He is also a noted speaker, preaching the Gospel to those where he is commissioned.

Mary Gaskins has a Master degree in Psychology and is preparing to embark on a discovery mission that will create a new branch of Behaviorism Psychology.

Steve has been married to his bride, Mary since 1998. They are the parents of six children. Together, they share the crown of ten grandchildren.

It is our sincere and modest hope that those reading this book will be blessed.

Steve Gaskins

A SPECIAL THANK YOU TO YOU!!!!!

Please send your thoughts and

constructive criticism and/or sign up to

receive newsletters and special emails

walkingwithjesus@gmx.com